Fifties Stylish American Cars

DECADE OF DAZZLE

Photography by Henry Rasmussen

Motorbooks International
Publishers & Wholesalers Inc
Osceola, Wisconsin 54020, USA   ®

First published in 1987 by Motorbooks International Publishers & Wholesalers Inc., PO Box 2, 729 Prospect Avenue, Osceola, WI 54020 USA

Motorbooks International is a certified trademark, registered with the United States Patent Office

Printed and bound in Hong Kong

The information in this book is true and complete to the best of our knowledge. All recommendations are made without any guarantee on the part of the author or publisher, who also disclaim any liability incurred in connection with the use of this data or specific details

Library of Congress
  Cataloging-in-Publication Data
ISBN 0-87938-249-X

Motorbooks International books are also available at discounts in bulk quantity for industrial or sales-promotional use. For details write to Special Sales Manager at the Publisher's address

On the cover: A 1953 Hudson Hornet club coupe, captured on the beach at Daytona, Florida. **On the back cover:** A 1956 Thunderbird, photographed on Governors Island, New York. **On the frontispiece:** The stately frontal features of a 1953 Cadillac Eldorado used by Ike in the presidential inauguration parade. **On the title page:** A close-up of the Hornet posterior forms a nostalgic reminder of the days when round was beautiful and chrome was plentiful. **On the last page:** The timeless elegance of the Continental is illustrated by the restrained styling of its wheel cover. **On this page:** The wheel of a 1953 Oldsmobile 88, photographed on the boardwalk at Coney Island, New York.

Contents

Introduction

Era of magnificent excess

Throughout the history of the American automobile, there has never been a decade like the fifties. Not that it produced the best and most beautiful of cars. That characterization is generally reserved for the thirties, the era of the great classics. Nor can one accuse the period of bringing forth the worst and ugliest. Posterity may well bestow that dubious distinction on the seventies, with its blatant disregard for craftsmanship and stumbling attitude toward styling.

No, the fifties is remembered as the era of excess, as the period when both manufacturers and consumers—in a frenzy of self-indulgence—threw dignity and discipline overboard.

However, this epitaph is primarily applicable to the last part of the era. The early days were indeed characterized by a serious search for new and worthwhile direction, as were many subsequent efforts by individual designers and manufacturers. But even the most excessive of creations conceived during the period as a whole resulted in automobiles that we, today at least, consider exceptional objects of nostalgia.

In the end, the automobiles from the era of chrome cornucopia, of fins and wings and portholes and kaleidoscopic color schemes, of lower and longer and wider bodies, of panoramic windshields and autronic eyes and ultramatic drives, have endeared themselves to the mainstream of enthusiasts like no others.

And while these products of unchecked imagination are certainly not looked upon with the dignified admiration of the classics, they are

Above: Peace unleashes a longing to see the country—1949 Kaiser Traveler with trailer in South Dakota's Badlands. **Right:** New trends in styling—Raymond Loewy and his 1953 Studebaker Starliner.

embraced with a warm and heartfelt affection, the kind of emotion brought forth by spontaneous displays of passion.

The forces responsible for generating the movements of this memorable decade were numerous in number and varied in scope. They can be categorized in currents of a general, as well as of an individual, nature. And although there were certainly broad and enduring tendencies present, such as the one that dictated the gradual increase in the size of the automobile, there were also narrow trends—fashions that blossomed, but faded quickly, like the dead branches of a tree.

The source of the strongest of the general forces was the war—and the ensuing peace. As is certainly the case with periods of depravation in any country, be it food or money, the end of the "dark age" invariably brings excess.

During the war, automotive desires had from necessity been kept in check. Then, in 1946, when production was started up again, there was simply not enough cars to go around. After a beginning pace that produced just over three million units that first year, there was a gradual increase, until a new all-time record was set in 1949, with over six million cars placed on the road. The incredible energy of the market is illustrated by the fact that this figure rose to eight million the following year.

The slogan "Peace and Prosperity" was indeed the verbal manifestation of a magical force that managed to hold its spell throughout the fifties. A new all-time record was set in 1955, when the nine-million mark was broken. Altogether, the fifties produced nearly sixty million cars.

However, the pent-up desires of the postwar consumer did not translate only into a tremendous increase in production, but also—as the euphoria developed and became ripe with excess—into a degeneration of values. In other words, while in the beginning a purchase was dictated by a desire to be mobile, for the purpose of seeing the country, for instance, these desires were in time replaced by motives of shameless vulgarity, such as a need to outshine one's neighbor. Psychologists even began talking about the automobile as an expression of repressed sexuality —cars were big and brutally potent.

But so much for general forces.

The individual who, through his dynamic personality, became the most dominant force during the early postwar era was Harley Earl, the head of styling at General Motors. Beginning his career in the late twenties, throughout the thirties he

Above: The jet age arrives—first to join the Air Force is the Lockheed F-80 Shooting Star, deployed in 1945. **Right:** Aircraft design provides inspiration for stylists—the taillight of a 1953 Oldsmobile 88.

laid the foundation for the direction automotive styling would take after the war. A design such as Buick's 1937 Y-Job, the first experimental show car, was an obvious leader in this respect. He continued to display his flair for fashion in a long series of show cars, with the 1951 Le Sabre exemplifying a worthy culmination.

Earl is credited with bringing aircraft themes into automotive styling. As early as 1941, so the story goes, the US Air Force P-38 fighter became the inspiration for fins, bombs and spears. Under Earl's direction, General Motors managed to attain a standing of undisputed leadership in styling, a position that would last well into the fifties.

Another influential individual, although he lacked Earl's broadness of base, was Frank Spring, who created the 1948 Hudson Hornet. His inspiration can also be said to have emanated from circumstances connected with the war, since the miracle of wartime progress—especially as it pertained to aircraft technology—had spawned the anticipation that great new themes could be expected when production of cars would finally be resumed.

The truth of the matter was that relatively little development had taken place during the war, a reality underscored by the fact that the cars brought out in 1946 were virtually identical to those of 1942.

This utopian state of anticipation had been fueled by a variety of artists, whose illustrations—drawing purely on imagination—had been published in a number of speculative articles. These designs indicated that the postwar automobile would be round and smooth, like a bathtub turned upside-down, and that the window areas would be expansive, allowing a spectacular view of the landscape one so much longed to see.

In addition to being adopted by Hudson, this style was also embraced

Above: Men of influence—General Motors styling chief Bill Mitchell and Buick stylist Ned Nickles iron out details. **Right:** Proprietary pride—Continental creator William Clay Ford poses with his car.

by Lincoln-Mercury, Packard and Nash-Rambler. While certainly successful at first, particularly as it was expressed in the Hudson, this fashion soon faded—a dead branch.

A fashion with staying power, although just a small detail, was introduced by Ned Nickles. A designer under Harley Earl, Nickles was responsible for the creation of Buick's portholes. This prestige item was certainly not an unimportant factor in the phenomenal popularity of the marque. First seen in 1949, the portholes could be found on Buicks in one form or another for years to come—except in 1958 and 1959.

Another distinguishing fashion element of the era, one that has taken on symbolic proportions, was the tail fin. While, as noted, it was initiated by Harley Earl, Chrysler stylist Virgil Exner was the man responsible for turning it into the fad it ultimately became. Although there were indeed fins present on his 1956 creations, it was on the 1957 models that they first reached prominence. Combined with the clean new look of these cars, Exner's fins touched off a furious battle of catch-up among the manufacturers.

The fact that this craze in the end got out of hand, with Chrysler being one of the worst offenders— the fin on the 1960 models stretched as far as the front door—was a development for which Exner, who by then had left Chrysler, expressed deep disappointment.

Yet another individual conspicuously connected with the era is Raymond Loewy. He was one of the foremost of a handful of industrial designers who in the thirties began to reshape the fashion awareness of the American consumer with, for instance, streamlined household appliances.

Loewy's first postwar contribution to automobile styling was the 1947 Studebaker. With its enormous wraparound rear window, it was yet another interpretation of the utopic themes in vogue at the time. His solution for the front end of the 1950 Studebaker—with its prominent spinner grille—has become one of the classics of the era.

In 1953 Loewy struck again, this time in the form of the beautiful Studebaker Starliner. The fact that

Above: Early days of racing—cars line up for start on the beach of Daytona in 1954. **Left:** Ostentation becomes the norm—gold and glitter makes for a flashy instrument panel on Packard's 1955 Caribbean.

this direction in styling ultimately also became a dead branch might have had more to do with the troubles within the company, and with market forces in general, than with the design in particular.

There were indeed many other illustrious individuals who helped shape the face of the fifties—unfortunately too numerous to name—as there indeed were other forces of a general nature that deserve at least a passing mention, such as the hot-rodders and the customizers, as well as the sports car and racing scenes.

As the fifties came to a close, so did the era of magnificent excess. The next decade brought more indulgence, to be sure, but was anticlimactic—it became the era of appalling excess.

But, perhaps, in the end, what really makes the difference is not so much the sum of educated opinions as the simple truth of personal preferences. In that respect we can all demand forgiveness for having been influenced by that time-honored master of persuasion, nostalgia.

Today, as the disagreements over the shape of fins and spears and grilles have become virtually irrelevant, we can indulge ourselves by retreating to our favorite armchair to enjoy a look at the nostalgic scenes on the pages of this book.

Shown here is a subjective selection, to be sure, and one that was determined by the simple limitations of space. But the viewer will nevertheless be able to become reacquainted with many of the most prominent machines of the era. Regardless of their financial and critical success, or lack of, these creations have all earned their place in automotive history, as well as in the hearts of enthusiasts of every persuasion.

Above: Peace and prosperity—happy days bring a new love affair with old favorites, the automobile and the gas station. **Left:** Stylists go overboard—the elaborate chrome spear of a 1959 Ford Skyliner.

1953 Hudson Hornet

Styling, step-down and sting

The Hudson Hornet owed its phenomenal success primarily to three basic elements. The first was its unique styling, the second was its innovative step-down chassis and the third was its powerfully potent engine.

The spaceship look was the work of Frank Spring, whose unique background combined both engineering and styling. Spring had designed a complete car in 1921—including the engine. In 1923, he had moved to a coach-building firm, where he created the shapes for both automobiles and airplanes. In charge of Hudson styling between 1931 and 1955, Spring certainly played one of the main leads in the Hudson saga.

The step-down chassis also emanated from the imaginative mind of Frank Spring. He had first proposed the idea in 1941.

The prototype had its frame running on the outside of the rear wheels, thereby allowing the floor to be as low as eight inches off the ground (thus the step-down reference). This in

Above: Winning combination—Hudson Hornet driver Dick Rathman becomes one of the most successful on the stock-car circuit. **Right:** Back where it belongs—the Hornet revisits the beach at Daytona.

turn made possible the ground-hugging sweep of the body.

One of the first new cars introduced after the war, the Hudson Commodore, arrived in December 1947. At that time, two six-cylinder engines were available: One was the old L-head; the other, a new 262 ci Super Six unit, producing 121 hp. But with General Motors introduction of V-8 power in 1949, Hudson desperately needed a new weapon.

Since the company did not have a V-8, the Super Six was bored out to 308 ci and tuned to produce 145 hp—ten more than Oldsmobile's V-8. When the Twin-H option—sporting two Carter carburetors and producing 170 hp—was introduced in 1951, the Hornet became the undisputed champion of both road and track.

Shown above, the round rear of the 1953 Hudson Hornet. The stylists, in an attempt to combine and unify, had now tied together bumper, taillights, name badge and license plate frame into one massive conglomerate of curving chrome. On the first model year, in 1948, the taillights were small and vertical, and mounted high on the fenders. The style shown in this picture was introduced in 1952. In 1954, the Hornet grew fins—these became the location of the taillights—and the classic Hornet look was lost.

Initial sketches called for a slab-sided body that enveloped both front and rear wheels. In the end this approach was deemed too advanced, and the front wheels received conventional openings. The side of the body was decorated with just a simple crease that ran the entire length of the panel. In 1951, a chrome spear was added below the crease. In 1952, the spear was lifted, covering the crease, and finished off by a flourish of chrome. This expression of creative joy, as seen in the picture to the right, became even more prominent for 1953.

Previous page
On the previous spread, a 1953 Hudson
Hornet club coupe photographed on the
beach at Daytona. This exquisite example
belongs to Chuck Jones of Silver Springs,
Florida, who also performed the painstaking
restoration. The car stands on a portion of
the exact stretch of beach that made up one
of the straightaways when the Hudsons were
raced there in the late forties and early
fifties. Legend has it that a number of cars
were lost in the waves and are still buried in
the sand below that unruly surface.

Shown on this spread, a portion of the Hudson's dash. At first located on either side of the center-mounted radio, the speedometer and clock—which were twins, as far as styling was concerned—were moved to a position ahead of the driver. Also, the dash was painted the color of the exterior, rather than using simulated woodgrain as on the early cars. Once comfortably seated inside the cabin of a Hudson, it didn't take driver and passengers long before they could imagine themselves transported to the fantasy world of Buck Rogers.

23

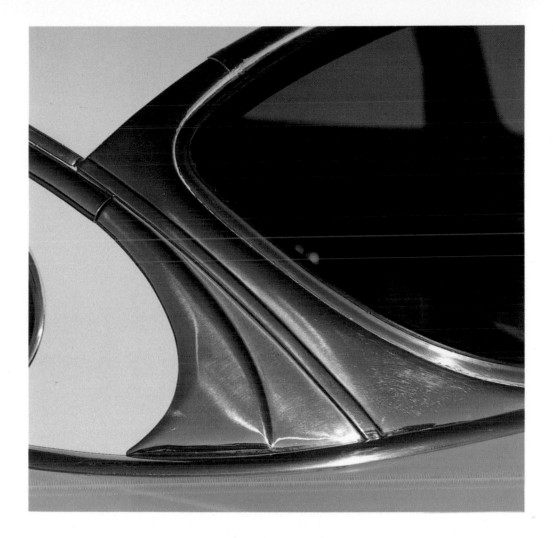

The spotlight and the sun visor were fashionable accessories of the era. Shocking colors and two-tone combinations also belonged to the picture of that period. The colors used on the feature car were referred to as Jefferson Green and Corinthian Creme. (The people who came up with the names seem to have been as imaginative as the ones who mixed the colors.) At least a dozen shades, and combinations of shades, were listed on the charts.

The item featured in the close-up above is an example of attention to detail, as well as a compliment to both the stylists and the consumers of an era when the sensuous pleasures of lines and curves were much appreciated. At the outset—in the late forties—the Hudson had been almost devoid of chrome, with the simple forms pressed into the metal being the only decorative elements. With the start of the chrome race, this philosophy gradually changed, but in the early fifties excess was still the exception.

1953 Cadillac Eldorado

Epitome of extravagant elegance

When Harley Earl in 1948 introduced a small fin on the Cadillac it was a daring move, with the marque having a rather conservative tradition. But the fin was small and it did indeed provide a tingling touch of excitement. As it turned out, the little item became a Cadillac trademark, staying virtually unchanged for eight years.

But what did not stay unchanged was the basic body—it was totally redesigned for 1950, becoming longer and lower. Changing also were grilles and bumpers, gradually becoming more menacing. In the end, the bumper guards protruded like huge battering rams.

For 1953, taking a clue from the Le Sabre show car, Earl introduced a wraparound windshield on a new, top-of-the-line convertible with a name that oozed richness—Eldorado.

The Eldorado was indeed rich—from its leather upholstery, wire wheels and concealed top, to its price tag of $7,750. The exclusivity factor was further

Above: Car for the famous—President Eisenhower waves from the Eldorado supplied to him for the inauguration parade. **Right:** Presidential history preserved—the same Eldorado three decades later.

underscored by a production of only 532 units.

For 1954, with $2,000 cut off the price tag, sales rose to 2,150 units. The 1955 model—sporting big tail fins—sold even better, 3,950 units. It was the only model in the Cadillac line to have those fins. And, as was the case with the wraparound windshield, the Eldorado heralded the future—a few years later, Cadillac had fins that put a jet fighter to shame.

However, in spite of the excesses Cadillac managed to maintain a certain dignity—an outrageous elegance—and whenever an example of those big convertibles is encountered today, there is an instant connection with those carefree, cloud-nine days that characterized this era of optimism.

The Eldorado was brought out in commemoration of Cadillac's fiftieth anniversary, thus the golden chevron, found not only up front but on the rear deck lid as well, as seen in the photograph on this spread. The exterior of the automobile did not carry any reference to the Eldorado name. Notice the gigantic bumper guards, whose styling was inspired by the shape of bombs. The Eldorado was available in only four standard colors that first year: Aztec Red, Azure Blue, Alpine White and Artisan Ochre. The top came in white or black, and was made from Orlon.

Next page
The scene on the following spread is graphic proof of the fact that the Eldorado stood lower than the standard Cadillacs. Not only had the beltline been dropped about one inch, but the suspension had also been modified, both measures resulting in a lowering of about three to four inches. Assembled on the regular production lines, the Eldorado did require a certain amount of hand work, however, especially in the area of the cut-down doors. This particular example, owned by Leo Gephardt of Dayton, Ohio, is the second unit built, and was used by President Eisenhower during the inauguration parade.

Pictured on this spread, the sumptuous interior of the 1953 Eldorado. The leather upholstery came in three colors, depending on the exterior: red, blue and black, with white, ribbed inserts. There were faired-in armrests and two-way power seats. Futher standard equipment included Hydra-matic transmission, power steering, dual heater and windshield washers. Note, in the picture to the left, the special cover—on this early example it was made from fiberglass—which allowed the top to fully disappear.

A special item of interest in the picture above is the white hand-grip insert on the steering wheel. This item was unique to the Eldorado, as were the door pulls, the leather-padded dash and the design of the instrument panel. As noted, the Eldorado name was not displayed on the exterior—but it is found here, on a dash-mounted plaque. The radio—standard equipment— represented the latest in the field, with its signal-seeking and preselector capabilities. Also standard were power-operated windows, as well as the small windwings attached to the wraparound windshield.

1953 Studebaker Starliner

Commander of The Continental Look

The 1953 Studebaker Starliner, as seen from the viewpoint of styling, represents the best of the era. With its low, lean and refreshingly clean lines the design exudes discipline —a rare virtue in the fifties.

Raymond Loewy must be given the ultimate credit for this look, since the Studebaker was conceived under his direction. But the actual idea originated with Bob Bourke, one of the stylists on his staff. Seeing Bourke's original sketches, Loewy was intrigued, and encouraged the creation of a full-scale model, with Bourke and another stylist, Bob Koto, each working out one side. In the end the Bourke side was chosen, and so was born the style Loewy and Studebaker called "The Continental Look."

But this design, a coupe— in production form called the Starliner (pillarless) and the Starlight (with pillar)—almost missed the boat. Intended as a show car, its basic shape was translated into a sedan, which was approved for manufacture.

Above: Gas mileage champion—a Studebaker Land Cruiser crosses the finishing line after a three-day run from Los Angeles to Sun Valley, Idaho. **Right:** Unadorned beauty—the 1953 Studebaker Starliner.

But Loewy kept pushing for the coupe to be built as well. Studebaker finally agreed. However, the decision came so late that early examples were marred by sloppy assembly.

The 1953 Studebaker was powered by a new V-8. In its basic layout it resembled the design introduced by Cadillac and Oldsmobile in 1949. But the Studebaker unit, with its 232 ci, was smaller and lighter— by thirteen pounds. It produced 120 hp, and a top speed of 95 mph.

Unfortunately, the pure shape of the Starliner was soon compromised. First weighted down by a more elaborate grille as well as a chrome spear down the side, a final addition of fins constituted the ultimate humiliation of this fifties classic.

Previous page
The photograph on the previous spread illustrates the clean, flowing lines of the 1953 Studebaker Starliner. The simplicity is unmarred by chrome and other distracting embellishments. Notice that the monotony of the side panel—which the lack of these decorations could otherwise have caused—is delicately broken by that smoothly sweeping curve pressed directly into the steel. In this scene the windows have been rolled down, illustrating the appearance the stylist had originally intended. (His first efforts specified that the door end farther back, thus eliminating the need for a quarter window.)

The scene on this spread shows the interior of the 1953 Studebaker Starliner. The original specifications were arrived at after including an unusual (for the time) amount of consideration for safety. These called for both a padded dash and a padded steering wheel. Unfortunately, in the end, cost considerations ruled out these features. Another original idea that also fell victim to the bean counter's ax was a separate bucket seat for the driver, supplemented by a bench for the two front passengers. Instead, as can be seen, a full bench became the substitute.

Although the use of a wide-angle lens in the photographs on this spread causes some unpleasant distortion, especially in the three-quarter angle above, the pictures do illustrate the fact that, regardless of vantage point, the 1953 Studebaker Starliner looked exciting, pleasing and harmonious—character traits of a true masterpiece. This particular example was photographed in the desert near Palm Springs, California. The owner is Tom Hines of Reseda, California.

A most unique feature on the Starliner was the reverse angle of the fenders. Here Bob Bourke is thought to have been inspired by aircraft designs. The Lockheed Constellation airliner in particular, it is said, was a favorite of his. Although most designs suffer in the translation from clay to metal, Bourke had reason to be pleased in the case of his Starliner. A couple of details, however, were ultimately compromised—the taillight bezels and the rear bumper were separate on the finished product, but one smooth unit in Bourke's clay.

1953 Buick Skylark

Monument to a master of imagination

In 1940, General Motors' dynamic styling chief, Harley Earl, brough in a new talent, whose creative mind produced ideas as bright and numerous as fireworks on the Fourth of July. His name was Ned Nickles. Having no formal education beyond high school, his only letter of recommendation consisted of the fact that he had been drawing cars since he was five. Yet, the influence of Ned Nickles would be felt for years to come.

To begin with, Nickles was put to work on advanced styling proposals for Chevrolet. But in 1945, he was put in charge of Buick, a marque he would change to such a degree that it became one of the style leaders. His influence was first seen in the 1949 models, which sported portholes and the first hardtop coupe—a first-rate trendsetter. Also, on late Rivieras of that year, he introduced the sweep spear—another winner.

However, Nickles soon went wild with chrome, creating the toothiest grilles in the

Above: A smile full of teeth—Buick chief stylist Ned Nickles creates the toothiest grille in the business. **Right:** Exercise in exclusivity—Nickles' 1953 Skylark becomes an instant collector car.

business—as in 1950. But it worked. Consumers loved it and translated their approval into purchases. From a total in 1946 of 160,000 units, Buick's production skyrocketed to three quarters of a million in 1955.

The Skylark was a luxurious limited-edition convertible brought out in commemoration of Buick's fiftieth anniversary in 1953. Here Nickles restrained himself, eliminating the portholes and slimming the sweep spear. Only 1,690 units were built. The Skylark was revised for 1954; it became shorter and lost some weight. Just 836 were produced—a truly limited edition. As such, the two Skylarks occupy a special place in Buick history, and are considered the rarest and most sought after of the Buicks from the fifties.

The rear of this particular 1953 Skylark featured in the photograph on this spread is accentuated by an aftermarket continental kit. The addition of the chunk of glitter, although certainly a counterbalance to the huge mass of chrome represented by the grille, is really a contradiction of Nickles' efforts to simplify the surfaces of the Skylark —something he did not dare to do on his bread-and-butter models, perhaps knowing too well what the public at large demanded. Photographed with a weathered hangar wall as a background, this survivor belongs to Deno Chronis, of Ann Arbor, Michigan.

Next page
The 1953 Skylark provided Ned Nickles with an opportunity to try out some of his advanced styling concepts. However, cost considerations demanded that he work with a body already in existence—he chose the Roadmaster convertible. Striving for a sleeker look, he decided to lower the beltline. He also designed a new chrome spear, thinner and more delicate and swept back across the rear wheelwell—now fully open to allow exposure of the wire wheels—and extended almost to the end of the rear fender. The sideview on the next spread shows the finished result. Note that Nickles did not use a wraparound windshield and that he had eliminated the portholes he had invented.

Nickles' first efforts after taking over responsibility for Buick styling centered around prestige items. The "bombsight" hood ornament came in 1946 and the revised grille the following year. Unchanged in 1948, the grille was made wider in 1949, and in 1950 Nickles unveiled his ultimate shocker. The teeth had taken a huge bite out of the bumper and it was either just the ticket—or too much. Apparently, the latter was the verdict at Buick, for the grilles gradually became a little less ferocious. Shown on the left, the 1953 version, used unchanged on the Skylark.

The bombsight hood ornament—decorating the 1953 Skylark above—had that year received its third revision. At first featuring just the ring with the bomb suspended in its center, it was changed in 1951, and featured the bomb connected with the hood through a long tail. In 1953 Buick introduced its new 322 ci V-8, a fact reflected in the new style, which now featured the bomb cradled in a prominent vee. Also new was a concave chrome foundation; this ingenius arrangement created a feeling of depth. In this configuration, the design became one of the best hood ornaments of the era.

1953 Oldsmobile 88

From staid sedan to radical rocket

The Oldsmobile 88 became the first high-performance car of the postwar period, and it meant a radical transformation of the marque, which went from sedate family car to spirited race-track champion in one season.

This metamorphosis was not so much the result of conscious image building as it was the logical effect of the 1949 introduction of the Rocket, a new, ninety-degree overhead-valve V-8, with a short stroke and wide bore. Created by Gilbert Burrell, its oversquare design represented a break with traditional thinking, and the implementation of this radical concept paid off in a most potent package. Displacement was 304 ci, and output was 135 hp at 3600 rpm. As the horsepower race heated up,

compression went from 7.25 in 1949 to 9.25 in 1956—when as much as 240 hp was extracted.

Right from the start in 1949, Oldsmobile dominated the NASCAR scene. And 1950 brought more of the same, plus an impressive overall win in the

Above: Dominating the racing scene—a pair of Oldsmobiles share the pole position at the start of the 1953 Daytona. **Right:** Open-air fun and frivolity—a 1953 Oldsmobile 88 convertible captured at Coney Island.

first Panamerican road race. Among all the publicity fallout from these successes, the news that the California Highway Patrol had decided to switch to the Rocket did not hurt the new Oldsmobile image one bit. In 1951 the NASCAR superiority reached a zenith—almost twice as many points were scored by Oldsmobile as the runner-up. Then came the Hornet, and by 1952 the golden days were over for Oldsmobile.

But if the racing victories were harder and harder to come by, the reputation garnered during those heady days of NASCAR dominance continued to translate into sales. In 1950, production had reached 268,000 units. The following year, this figure dipped to 185,000. But by 1953, it was up again, reaching a new high of 335,000.

The strong horizontal emphasis on the
Oldsmobile grille was evident already before
the war. In 1946, the theme was
strengthened through a distinctive design
that featured four horizontal bars, all with
decoratively downturned ends. While the
basic theme was continued in the 1948
restyling, two of the bars were removed. By
1953, as shown on the left, only the upper
bar retained the original curve; the second
bar was straight, and sported large bullet
designs in each end. The continental kit in
the picture above was an aftermarket item.

During the early years, 1949 to 1951,
Oldsmobile shared its basic shape with
Chevrolet. The visual separation of the two
was left up to the grille and a variety of trim
details. The classic Oldsmobile 88 came
from this period, certainly not because of its
kinship to Chevrolet, but because those
were the great years of racing glory. In 1952,
the Oldsmobile line received styling
modifications that placed it ahead of
Chevrolet as far as fashion was concerned.
The pictures on this spread show this new
style in 1953 trim.

Previous page
Parked in front of a Coney Island
delicatessen, which was no doubt stocked
with a wide assortment of epicurean delights,
the 1953 Oldsmobile 88 convertible—shown
in the picture on the previous spread—was
no less of an invitation to the taste buds
than was the cotton candy, cold beer and
hot pizza. The lines were well balanced,
with just a touch of fins and not too much
chrome—but enough to keep the eye
engaged. The 1953 version differed from the
previous year's when it came to the shape of
the trim just ahead of the rear wheel. While
this area in 1952 was the site of a huge
blotch of chrome, here it sported a smaller
trim piece that followed closely the slanting
angle set up by the upward-pointing tip of
the spear.

The scene on this spread communicates
with a certain blue-sky clarity that mood of
temptation—perhaps we should call it a
frivolous invitation to self-indulgence—
created by the colors and shapes of the
fifties. As if these sensual salvos where not
enough to soften the defenses of the buyers
of this era, there were more concrete
temptations of convenience a salesperson
could emphasize, such as power steering and
power brakes. And, for those concerned
with ride and handling, the well-informed
solicitor only had to mention the fact that
there were coil springs on all four wheels,
lever shocks, front and rear antiroll bars, and
not just one—but two—stabilizers!

Oldsmobile carried a rocket on the hood already in 1946, but with the 1948 introduction of the new Futuramic-style cars, it was fitted with long, swept-back wings. Thus, when the new Rocket engine was fired up in 1949, a fitting hood ornament was already in place. In 1950 the wings grew even longer. Finally, the 1952 restyling of the entire Oldsmobile line gave it wing-tip pods. The style was kept for 1953 and is shown above—very attractive indeed, with its sleek, speed-evoking lines. The beautifully restored Oldsmobile 88 featured on these pages belongs to Art Koenig of Mineola, New York.

The geometric pattern created by the planks of the Coney Island boardwalk—shown in the photograph to the right—makes for an intriguing contrast to the turbulent curvature created by the chrome and paint surfaces of the Oldsmobile. Images not reflected in these cold mirrors of steel include the swift shapes of the sea gulls, the slowly rotating outline of a Ferris wheel and the expression of nostalgia in the eyes of old Moe, caretaker of a Steeple Chase amusement stand down the alley.

1954 Chevrolet Corvette

Sheep in wolf's clothing

General Motors' flamboyant chief stylist, Harley Earl, must be credited with providing the spark that led to the creation of the first Corvette. His inspiration came from a desire to produce a car that would appeal both to the hot-rodders in California and the enthusiasts of the import racing scene with their MGs, Jaguars and Porsches.

Because the planned production run was short and time was of the essence, a new material—fiberglass—was chosen for the body. The actual shape was sculpted by Bob McLean, with Earl's influence clearly visible in the wraparound windshield and the small fins on the rear fender, both features of his 1951 Le Sabre show car.

The Corvette became the star of the New York Motorama

in 1953. But even though it looked smashing with its smooth and simple lines—which were closer to the Mercedes 300SL than the Jaguar XK120—under that skin hid an unexciting six-cylinder engine that had its origin in a 1941 Chevrolet truck unit.

Above: Space-age pleasure dome—an aftermarket plexiglass bubble is fitted to a handful of Corvettes in 1954. **Right:** The look that sends the ball rolling—a 1954 Corvette shows off its sensual curves.

For use in the Corvette, it had been souped up with high-lift cams and three carburetors but still did not generate any excitement. Adding to the insult was the fact that it was coupled to Chevrolet's two-speed automatic Powerglide transmission. The poor sales results experienced that first year proved that this approach indeed did not appeal to the sports car enthusiast.

However, the subsequent progress of the Corvette story has shown that the original idea had staying power. And although the mechanical features of that first Corvette left a lot to be desired, the styling was of such caliber that the image has indeed become something of a symbol to all Corvette enthusiasts.

Corvette creators Earl and McLean had originally envisioned plexiglass-covered headlights, a fact also suggested by the smooth shape of the fender. This feature was quite an advanced concept at the time, and had been used only on racing machines such as Jaguar's Le Mans-winning 1951 C-type. In the end the plexiglass was deemed too delicate for use on a production car—there were still a lot of dirt roads in those days. Instead, a decorative wire mesh—also racing inspired—was created. However, wire wheels, as shown in the photograph above, were not standard but an aftermarket item.

If one compares the front features of the first Corvette with those of other contemporary sports cars, the closest thing is the 300SL introduced by Mercedes-Benz in 1952. The Corvette had the same wide look as well as a similar front fender curve. The grille was also quite compatible—although more glamorous on the Corvette, with its toothy expression. A model of the 300SL was shown to the press on March 13, and the initial work on the Corvette took place during the month of April. Thus, while just a speculation, the link to the 300SL is possible.

The picture on this spread, photographed through a wide-angle lens, projects an awesome—and exaggerated—view of the ample hindquarters found on the early Corvette. This distortion of width and perspective amplifies the elements of speed and flight built into the design—those fenders with their small rocket fins and that round rear deck with its air-cheating smoothness. Notice that the twin exhaust pipes protruded through the rear portion of the body, and that the license plate recess was plexiglass-covered.

Next page
The photograph on the following spread
shows a sideview of the early Corvette. The
shape obviously represented the meeting of
two schools: One, the European, with its
classic simplicity was typified by the
unpretentious, unadorned flow of lines and
the geometrically straightforward wheelwells.
The other, the America, with its emphasis
on symbols was exemplified by the aircraft-
inspired wraparound windshield and the
spaceship-influenced tail fins. But the
Corvette soon found ways to express a styling
philosophy all its own. The pristine 1954
model pictured here belongs to Fred Neff of
Minneapolis, Minnesota.

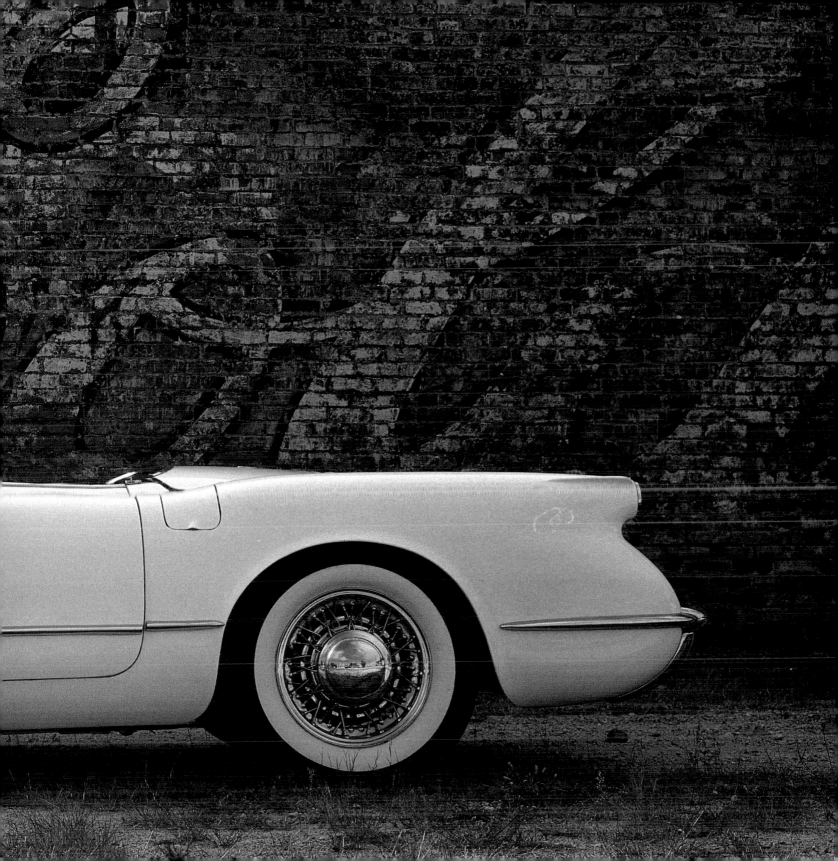

The feature car was photographed on the grounds of the old railroad depot in Minneapolis, with the city's sun-silhouetted skyline providing an ever-changing backdrop. Here the Corvette cockpit—with its all-surrounding chrome molding—appeared from its most inviting aspect. Certainly overstyled from a European viewpoint, the interior continued the aircraft theme of the exterior, with the speedometer, for instance, set in a propeller-inspired pod. The same shape reappeared on the passenger side—for symmetry—which here housed the speakers. Other gauges and controls were also organized symmetrically, certainly at the expense of practicality. A novelty was found in the larger dial at the center of the dash, which besides functioning as a tachometer, also recorded the number of hours the engine was in operation, as on an airplane. The shift lever, although located on the floor where it belonged, was something of a parody. As noted, it connected with a two-speed automatic transmission—certainly a most appalling affair. But the Corvette lived—and learned.

1955 Packard Caribbean

Dreamboat and sinking ship

Perhaps like no other car in the selection featured on the pages of this book, the Packard Caribbean illustrates the transformation of the American automobile in general—and, of course, Packard in particular. The contrast is especially apparent with the Packard heritage reaching so far back.

Imagine for a moment the Packard of the twenties and thirties, with the sleek hood and the narrow grille, its classic shape as good as a trademark. Then compare that image with the one on these pages, its dazzling cascades of glitter and its multitude of color rivaling a Christmas tree.

From its prewar eminence as one of the world's great marques, Packard's postwar reappearance clearly indicated a slow but gradual watering down of the ideals that had been the guiding light for so long.

By the time the Caribbean appeared, Packard was near the end of its rope. Still, the massive machine was quite a handful. It was longer than most, and

Above: In the public eye—Howard Hughes boards a plane after the abrupt postponement of a Senate investigation into his business practices. **Right:** Legacy of an eccentric—the Packard he drives only once.

heavier than most, and also had an engine to match. Power came from a 352 ci overhead-valve V-8 that produced 275 hp. With dual four-barrel carburetors, it was almost a hot rod. But all this power was necessary, as it had to extend not only to the wheels, but to a full complement of power accessories.

Keeping the comparison with the classic Packards in mind, one still cannot leave the subject of the Caribbean without using some adjectives of appreciation—for what it was meant to be, it was a magnificent automobile, an extravagant tribute to the era, and one brimming with nostalgia.

Finally, it should be pointed out that Caribbeans are very rare. Only 2,189 units were built between 1953 and 1956.

Previous page
The exotic location in the picture on the previous spread could very well represent the scenery in the rich, diplomatic district of a Caribbean island capital—the perfect setting for Packard's glamorous dreamboat, the Caribbean. But the location was actually Beverly Hills, California, another exotic playground, certainly not as fitting as far as the name is concerned but otherwise just as rich. Beverly Hills has always been home to this particular example, now owned by Stan Zimmerman. With less than 2,000 miles on the odometer it was not allowed to stray very far.

A present from Howard Hughes to Jean Peters, the eccentric industrialist's last wife, the Caribbean did not live up to its owner's expectations. First of all, Miss Peters did not like the white exterior—she had told Hughes to order the car painted a special green. Second, Hughes, a perfectionist, found fault with the carburetion, and had his mechanics make some alterations to the fuel lines, but to no avail. The Packard was stored away, but not forgotten. Thus, today we can enjoy the view of its perfectly pristine interior, as seen in the picture on this spread.

75

The Packard Caribbean certainly displayed a frontal view that contained all the fashionable elements of the day: the bullet-like bumper guards, the full-width grille (its Ferrari-inspired egg-crate pattern actually added a touch of class), the browed headlights, the V-8 chevron and a golden crest that rivaled anything that could be found on an aristocrat's smoking jacket. Although not functional, the twin air scoops decorating the hood gave an impression that ample power was available—which in fact was the case.

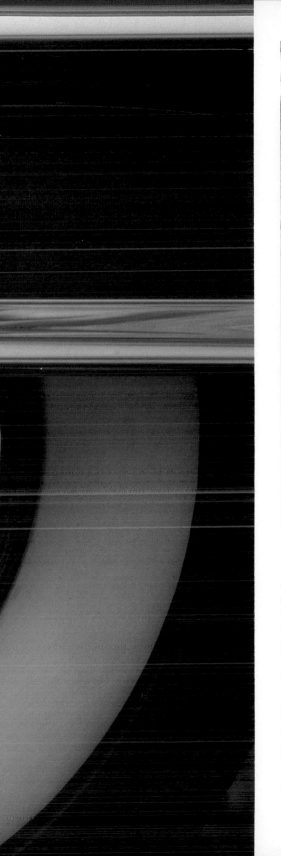

Although Packard by 1955 was indeed a sinking ship, the attention to detail and the workmanship displayed in its end-of-the-line products still gave a viewer reason to remember the good old days when Packard was the automobile from which other manufacturers took their cue. The scene to the left, although a trifle flamboyant with its shock of pink, still bred elegance, an effect accomplished by the use of only the simplest of lines. Even the center of the wheel cover carried a reminder of the classic era in the form of Packard's old hexagon, first used in 1904.

James Ward Packard—who, together with his brother William, was a founding father of the Packard automobile—passed away in 1928. In memory of Packard and his family's contribution to the marque, their coat of arms—which dates back to England and the times of knights—was adopted as a symbol. A cross of lozenges, surrounded by four roses, decorates the shield, while a pelican keeps watch from above. The pelican, sometimes also identified as a cormorant, crowned the radiator of Packard cars for decades, and was still put to good use on the 1955 Caribbean—as shown in the photograph above.

1956 Ford Thunderbird

The personal car personified

The Thunderbird represents both a gain and a loss. In contrast to Chevrolet, which bungled its introduction of the Corvette by confusing the public with sports car styling and family car engineering, Ford did it right to begin with—from the viewpoint of what it set out to create, the personal car. The fact that the Thunderbird had sports car performance, to some extent, was just a pleasant plus.

But while Chevrolet corrected its mistake by turning the Corvette into a true sports car, Ford went the other way, turning the Thunderbird into something that wasn't even a Thunderbird anymore, let alone a sports car. This was a double loss: first of the initial Thunderbird, then of the Corvette competitor it could have become.

The initial idea of a Ford sports car was first floated in 1951, but serious work did not begin until the Corvette made the idea ripe. The styling must be attributed to teamwork between Bob Maguire, David Ash, Damon Woods, Bill Boyer

Above: Birth of the Bird—press release photo from 1954 shows prototype with Fairlane badge still on the hood. **Right:** The personal car that breaks both hearts and sales records—a 1956 tours New York.

and others. The result was one of the best designs of the fifties. Its simplicity and strong emphasis on sweeping lines worked wonderfully well. Unfortunately, the original discipline was compromised in 1957, with the addition of the fins and the longer rear deck.

The Thunderbird was already, from the beginning, propelled by V-8 power. Displacement was 292 ci, output was 198 hp. Top speed was well over 100 mph.

Ford's personal car proved its point by selling phenomenally well—right from the start. In 1955, 16,155 units were built; in 1956, 15,631; and in 1957, 21,380. The Thunderbird also proved its mettle by becoming one of the most valuable and popular of all the collector cars of the fifties.

In 1955, Ford introduced new styling to its entire line of cars. It reflected the fashion of the day, which dictated longer, lower and wider bodies, wraparound windshields and, in addition to an abundance of chrome embellishments on the side panels, multicolor paint schemes. Throughout all this proliferation of new styling trends, Ford managed to keep a family resemblance—a look that was even transmitted to the new Thunderbird. The basic shape of the 1955 model was kept unchanged for 1956, except for the addition of a continental kit, as shown in the photograph on this spread.

Previous page

The clean crispness of the Thunderbird's styling is evident in the photograph on the previous spread. In retrospect, one can argue that the equipage would have looked even better without those oversize bumper guards that only serve to confuse the simple lines of the grille. However, one should be thankful for the fact that the stylists successfully fought the addition of a Fairlane-style sweep spear on the side panel—an idea that was strongly favored by top management. This would certainly have destroyed the forthright simplicity of the overall design.

The simplicity of the exterior line was carried through to the interior as well, as shown in the picture on this spread. A number of solutions were considered before the final one was arrived at, but in the end a need for economy dictated the use of as many standard components as possible, which was probably just as well, judging from styling sketches that depicted all kinds of elaborate designs. The good-looking floor-mounted lever connected to the Fordomatic automatic transmission. The well-preserved feature car was photographed on the Manhattan side of New York's Governors Island; it is owned by Ethan Allen Turner of Long Island, New York.

1956 Chrysler 300B

A blend of muscle and brains

Chrysler had grossly misjudged the styling trends that were to sweep the market in the early fifties. The company was thus left with a line that looked hopelessly outdated. Virgil Exner, the styling maestro, was brought in to put Chrysler back on track. And that he did—beginning in 1955. Suddenly there was excitement. The company called it "The Million Dollar Look." And the buyers agreed.

But Chrysler had another trick up its sleeve—the hemi V-8. Work on this engine had begun during the war, but peacetime brought it to completion, and in 1951 the hemi was put into action. However, its capacity was never fully realized until two men, Exner and Bob Rodger, a gifted development engineer, saw the potential for a great combination —thus was born the 300. This legendary machine became every bit as successful on the stock-car circuit as the Oldsmobile 88 and the Hudson Hornet had been during their golden years.

An intriguing aspect of the

Above: Record breaker on the run—the Daytona sand sees a 1955 Chrysler 300 cover the flying mile at 127 mph. **Right:** Improving the breed—the classic hood of the 1956 300B hides forty more horses.

300 was that it combined classic sedan styling with hot-rod power—much like Mercedes-Benz and its 300SEL would do more than ten years later. The 300, with its 300 hp engine, could reach 60 mph in ten seconds, and had a top speed of 130 mph.

In 1956, the 300B received Exner's tentative fins, which unfortunately disturbed the classic styling heritage. However, this was compensated for by the presence of another 40 hp under the hood.

Both trends—fins and horsepower—would figure in the making of the 1957 300C. With 390 hp inside its belly, the new 300 flew like a bullet. For the collector, the choice becomes a matter of priorities— some models have more brains, others have more muscle.

Previous page
The scene on the previous spread, showing a 300B making a pit stop at a gas station in Glendale, California, provides a perspective of the effect created by the introduction of fins to the 1956 model. The larger taillights and the use of chrome to connect the bezels with the bumper resulted in a definite distortion of the rear. But all this was part of an unstoppable trend. In addition to red, as seen on this particular example, owned by Singer Richard Carpenter, white and black were the only other exterior colors available. All had tan leather upholstery.

In the picture on this spread, the camera peeked through the rear portion of the pillarless window featured on the 300B, focusing attention on its busy dash. Partially obscured by the steering wheel was the pushbutton control box through which the PowerFlite transmission was operated. The steering effort was quite a handful, which underscored the fact that this was indeed a man's car. However, power steering was available as an option, as were power brakes, power seats and power windows. Heater and radio were other options, as was air-conditioning, beginning in 1956.

Previous page
The 300 was indeed a limited edition—only 1,692 units were built in 1955, and as few as 1,050 in 1956. These short runs made it economically unfeasible to produce special body panels; thus Exner had to choose from available components. The Newport two-door hardtop, which rested on a 126 inch wheelbase, provided the basics. The 1956 300B, as seen on the previous spread, is equipped with the wire wheel option. Under the hood, the option to have that year was the hemi in supertune, producing 355 hp. In this configuration, the 300B did 0-60 mph in under nine seconds and topped out at 140 mph.

The pictures on this spread show details of Exner's frontal treatment of the 300B. The grille came from the top-of-the-line Imperial. Fortunately, Exner did not specify the Imperial's overdramatic parking light bezels, which were integrated with the bumper, but chose to stay with the same items he had used in 1955. A further tribute to simplicity was the absence, both years, of the hood ornaments that adorned other cars in the line. The emblem, with its checkered-flag motif, received a letter addition signifying that this indeed was the second generation of the 300.

1956 Lincoln Continental Mark II

Too superb to survive

Seldom has automotive history seen a more ambitious project than the one that produced the Continental Mark II. Some of the company's brightest brains, directed by no less than a genuine Ford—William Clay Ford, one of Henry's grandsons—gave this effort the prime of their talents.

The origins of the Continental can be traced to Ford's desire to topple Cadillac from its position as "Standard of the World." Thus, the purpose was not to make money—this was ruled out from the beginning—but to build prestige.

William Clay Ford decided to pit five groups of stylists against one another, among them Ford's own, headed by John Reinhart. Purely on its own merits, one of the in-house proposals won, and the production process began. A young man of taste and ability, Ford was not one to direct from behind a desk, but involved himself in the actual work, to the point of sometimes laying clay with his own hands.

Above: Details make the whole—project chief William Clay Ford points out crucial area on clay model. Stylist John Reinhart listens. **Right:** Timeless styling—a 1956 Continental in a suitably elegant setting.

The result was one of the purest and most dignified designs of any era. This, coupled with the best in engineering, materials, equipment and craftsmanship, placed the Continental ahead of anything Cadillac—and anybody else—had to offer.

But while the product met the mark, sales did not. Only 4,660 units were built during the two model years, at a loss of $1,000 each. But the lack of profit was not the problem. The problem was that the car's high price limited the number of buyers to a narrow segment, and that segment was quickly saturated. Thus, to the deep disappointment of its creators and many a connoisseur came the early unmerited demise of one of America's finest automobiles.

Previous page

Although every other automobile on the market—even the products emanating from a distinguished marque like Packard—suffered from the stylist's preoccupation with chrome and fins and a variety of airplane paraphernalia, the designers of the Continental kept their creation as clean and subtle as was appropriate for a masterpiece in the classic tradition. The particular example displayed in the photograph on the previous spread is the property of William Clay Ford. His desire to own and preserve one of these cars is evidence enough of his feelings for the creation that was so much a result of his personal efforts.

Only the finest materials were used for the interior of the Mark II, shown in the picture on this spread, which was photographed on the Ford estate in Grosse Pointe Shores, Michigan. The dash was the object of much study, with locomotive and aircraft cockpits providing initial inspiration. One of the designs, later discarded, called for an instrument panel split into two levels. In the end, a very simple layout won out—so simple in fact that it perhaps comes across as lacking somewhat in distinction. But the sophisticated driver lacked nothing—a full complement of power equipment was standard.

Previous page
The frontal view of the Continental Mark
II, as captured in rapidly evaporating evening
light on the previous spread, makes for a
marvelous display of simplicity, elegance,
symmetry; in fact, every word associated
with taste found in the dictionary. Notice
the flat nacelles located at the ends of the
bumper. While certainly not the most ideal
objects to use for initial contact with other
cars, they served beautifully—from the
viewpoint of design—as a location for the
parking lights, which otherwise would have
been placed on the body, thus marring the
simplicity.

The view to the left, featuring the
Continental Mark II from behind, is as
impressive as the one from the front, seen
on the previous spread. The same flawlessness
of the basic line is found here, although the
simplicity has been compromised somewhat
in the application of the name and symbol.
Note the repetition of the nacelles at the
ends of the bumper—here they served as
exhaust outlets. Pictured above, the
Continental hood ornament, which was a
last-minute design. And although it had
been created without an eye toward the
Mercedes star, the German car maker was
not particularly pleased.

1957 Chevrolet Bel Air

The finest of all time

Like the other major automakers, General Motors began postwar production without fanfare—it was a seller's market anyway. Thus, in 1945, the Chevrolets of that year looked the same as the ones marketed in 1942. Still, they could not be built fast enough to keep up with demand.

But neither peace nor easy pickings would last. As the market became saturated, a new war was declared—that among the automakers. Styling and horsepower were two of the most formidable of the weapons used to win the favor of the buyers.

When the new Chevrolet arrived in 1949, it certainly looked more modern, although not radically so. There was, for instance, still a definite separation between front and rear fenders. The 1953 facelift added more chrome, but it was not until 1955 that a new style suddenly grabbed the attention of both young and old. However, by now the front line was moving fast, and drastic changes were introduced every year. The

Above: Pretty faces—the 1956 Chevrolet gets a new grille, a new bumper, new guards and new chrome. **Right:** Hard choices—the 1957 gets its face worked over again. It's the look that's hard to forget.

moderately sized grille of 1955, for instance, grew to full width in 1956.

Then, in 1957, came the Chevrolet that will live on as one of the most-loved symbols of the era. The grille became powerfully massive, a unit with the bumper; the fins were provocatively prominent; and the entire machine grew longer by another four inches. As a final touch, that year saw the introduction of fuel injection. With the 283 ci for the first time producing matching horsepower, the classic Chevrolet had arrived.

Just after the war, the carmaker glorified its product as "The Finest Chevrolet of All Time." Most enthusiasts, however, agree that the company should have waited a decade to introduce that slogan.

If one must have fins, well, then the ones on the 1957 Chevrolet—as seen in the photograph on this spread—are as nice as they come. The flowing line created by these fins, accentuated by the brushed and polished aluminum rear quarter panel inserts, becomes further exaggerated by the addition of the continental kit—a factory-installed option. The interior here features red vinyl upholstery with silver-gray circle pattern inserts, also of vinyl.

Next page

Jack Sessums—originally from the nation's capitol—became, as a result of his successful high-school graduation, the lucky owner of a 1957 Chevrolet. Even though the car itself soon passed on to other eager hands, the experience had made a lasting impression—one that nostalgia demanded be repeated. Now a resident of Redlands County, California, Jack happened to spot an example driven locally. Having obtained the beauty, he began a restoration that spanned several years. The result is the exquisite survivor in this feature, its perfect sideview decorating the following spread.

The view from the passenger seat of the
1957 Chevrolet—as seen in the photograph
on this spread—pleases the eye with a
delightful blend of form and color. The
convertible, while not the darling of the
street racers of the day—who favored the
two-door hardtop—has now become the
most collectible. If it, as is the case with
Sessums' example, is fitted with the $500
fuel-injection option, well, then it is the
ultimate—and not only because of the extra
performance, but because production was
limited.

Next page
The final photograph of the feature car
shows a fascinating view of the Chevrolet's
ample fins, their skyward sweep
appropriately exaggerated by the use of a
wide-angle lens. The steeply inclined angle
of the rear cut-off was first seen on
Studebaker's Starliner. This car also used
chrome to frame the edge of the fins, a
detail further refined by the stylists. The
power-operated antenna was a most popular
option. Further excitement was derived from
the fact that the gas filler cap was hidden
behind the left taillight.

1959 Ford Skyliner

Rare, retractable and outrageous

The Skyliner did not tempt the true introvert. First, it was a convertible, which meant that driver and occupants were in full view—as were the goings-on in the cockpit. Second, the top—stored in the rear deck—was electrically operated, and the magic of this appearance and disappearance act was in itself such a fascinating drama that it could not be performed without attracting a crowd.

When Ford introduced this feature on its 1957 Skyliner, it was labeled as the "World's Only Hide-Away Hardtop." This was true in the sense that no other manufacturer offered such a novelty at the time. However, it was not true in the sense that it was the only contraption of its kind ever produced. Peugeot, for instance, marketed a successful limited-

edition version, called the "Transformable," two decades earlier.

The system adopted by Ford was originally developed by Continental, and was planned as a feature to be introduced in

Above: Searching for the winning combination—stylists line up models painted in many colors for executives to choose from. **Right:** Novelty that wears off—the hood fits in the trunk, but not the luggage.

connection with future expansion of the line. However, when the hopeless grandiosity of Continental's plans became apparent, it was felt that the $2 million development cost should be put to good use in some other way.

The first model year saw as many as 20,766 Skyliners placed on the road. With a $2,945 price tag, it cost $340 more than a regular convertible. The following year, it seems, the novelty had already begun to wear off—sales dropped to 14,713 cars. In 1959 came another drop—12,915 units were made that year.

Of these three models, the last year—with its outrageous styling constituting the perfect match for such an outrageous feature—is obviously the most sought after.

The interior of the 1959 Skyliner was every bit as glamorous as the exterior, with color-coordinated seats and dash, and chrome spears on the door panels. On the functional side, a switch under the steering column activated the top mechanism, a column shift lever communicated with the three-speed Cruiseomatic transmission, and both steering and brakes were power assisted. The gas pedal ruled over Ford's 352 ci, ninety-degree, overhead-valve V-8, which, breathing through a four-barrel Holley, produced an ample 300 hp.

The basis for the original Skyliner was Ford's 1957 Fairlane convertible, which received a complete redesign from the passenger compartment back. That year Ford stylists had introduced the short-hood/long-deck look. This was fortunate for the Retractable—the fenders and the rear deck only required a lengthening of three inches and the hood a shortening of less than four inches. As a result—although the Skyliner certainly looks more ungainly—the family resemblance did not suffer much. For 1958, the body received a styling overhaul. The 1959—shown above—got both a restyling of the body and a redesign of the top mechanism.

The photograph to the left captures the magical moment. It took ten power relays, ten limit switches, eight circuit breakers, four lock motors and three drive motors—in addition to 610 feet of electrical wire—to run the show. And not only was the retractable top a spectacle to watch, it was surprisingly reliable. The factory claimed it had been tested for 10,000 cycles. However, a serious drawback was the fact that the top and its mechanism left limited space for luggage. The particular example featured here—exquisitely restored—belongs to Drexel Pentz of Grampian, Pennsylvania.

The photographs on the two previous spreads show the frontal and rear aspects of the 1959 Skyliner. Having expressed themselves fairly moderately in 1955 and 1956, the stylists went wild in 1957. The party continued through 1959, when, for instance, both Chevrolet and Ford extended the fins to the rear panel. The former featured wildly flopping wings, while the latter showed a degree of discipline, using straight lines and circles as a basis for the design. Admittedly, in the midst of all this excess one can find numerous details of beauty—an example is shown in the picture above.

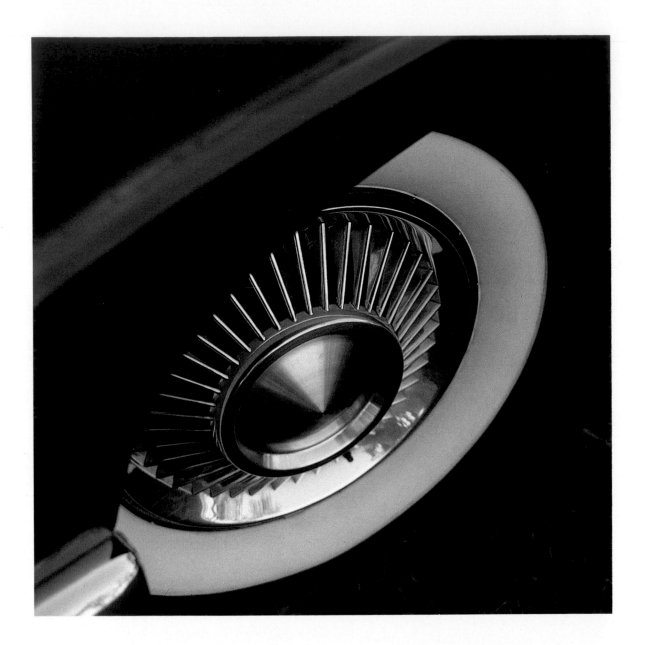